THE WORK OF HEROES: FIRST RESPONDERS IN ACTION

ANIMAL CONTROL
OFFICERS *to the* RESCUE

by **Meish Goldish**

Consultant: Officer Todd Stosuy
Field Services Manager
Santa Cruz County Animal Shelter
Santa Cruz, California

BEARPORT
PUBLISHING

New York, New York

Credits

Cover and Title Page, © Patricia Beck/Associated Press; TOC, © iStockphoto/Thinkstock; 4, © Reseda Mickey; 4TR, © Bronson Waite; 5, © Salina Journal, Salina, Kansas; 6, © Salina Journal, Salina, Kansas; 7BL, © Salina Journal, Salina, Kansas; 7TR, © Salina Journal, Salina, Kansas; 8, © Elisha Page/Associated Press; 9, © John Welsh/Riverside County Animal Services; 10, © Katie Selden/Associated Press; 11, © JAKE MAY/The Register-Mail; 12, © Susumu Kishihara; 13TR, © From The Daily Journal, 6/26 © 2012 The Daily Journal. All rights reserved. Used by permission and protected by the Copyright Laws of the United States. The printing, copying, redistribution, or retransmission of this Content without express written permission is prohibited; 13BR, © robag/Shutterstock; 14 © Pat Holm; 15, © Janet Begley, Scripps Treasure Coast Newspapers; 16, © Charles Holt, Advantage Wildlife Removal Cincinnati, OH; 17, © Elisha Page/Associated Press; 18, © ZUMA Press, Inc. / Alamy; 19, © Village of Oak Park/Illinois; 20, © John Badman/Associated Press; 21, © © Rose Palmisano/The Orange County Register/ZUMAPRESS.com; 22, © ZUMA Press/Newscom; 23, © The Blade/ Amy E. Voigt; 24L, © Annette Shaff/Shutterstock; 24R, © Jacqueline Lynch; 25, © Michael Cavazos; 26, © Jonathan Weiand/Associated press; 27, © ZUMA Press/Newscom; 28TL, © ZUMA Press/Newscom; 28TR, © MDC Exports; 28C, © Midwest Tongs.com; 28BL, © Keit Kangro / Alamy; 28BR, © D. Hurst / Alamy; 29TL, © Dave Hamman; 29TR, © Dave Hamman; 29B, © Kyodo News/Newscom; 31, © ZUMA Press/Newscom; 32, © PATRICK KELLEY/Associated Press.

Publisher: Kenn Goin
Senior Editor: Joyce Tavolacci
Creative Director: Spencer Brinker
Design: Debrah Kaiser
Photo Researcher: Picture Perfect Professionals, LLC

Library of Congress Cataloging-in-Publication Data

Goldish, Meish.
 Animal control officers to the rescue / by Meish Goldish.
    p. cm. — (The work of heroes : first responders in action)
 Includes bibliographical references and index.
 ISBN 978-1-61772-747-4 (library binding) — ISBN 1-61772-747-4 (library binding)
 1. Animal welfare—United States—Juvenile literature. I. Title.
 HV4764.G65 2013
 636.08′32—dc23
                         2012033460

For more information, write to Bearport Publishing Company, Inc., 45 West 21st Street, Suite 3B, New York, New York 10010. Printed in the United States of America.

10 9 8 7 6 5 4 3 2 1

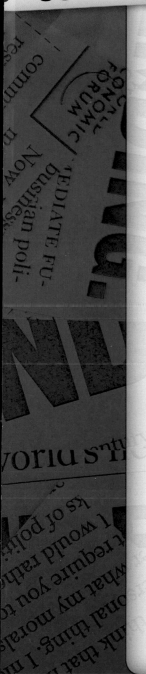

CONTENTS CONTENTS CONTENTS CONTENTS

CONTENTS CONTENTS

On Thin Ice

It was a winter evening in 2008. Gabe Seim and a friend were walking their dogs near a frozen pond at Indian Rock Park in Salina, Kansas. Suddenly, Gabe's dog, Porter, bolted onto the pond. The ice under Porter's feet broke, and the black Labrador plunged into the chilly water. Porter tried to crawl back onto the ice, but it was too slippery for his paws to grip.

Indian Rock Pond in warmer weather

Gabe rushed onto the icy pond to try to save Porter. However, the ice gave way, and he also fell into the water. After climbing out and returning to **shore**, Gabe called 911. The 911 operator quickly contacted Jane Trostle, an animal control officer, who sped to the scene. When she arrived, Porter had been in the freezing water for more than ten minutes. Could she save the dog in time?

A person can generally survive in extremely cold water for 10 to 20 minutes. The amount of time a dog can survive depends on the type of dog and its size.

Porter grew tired as he fought to keep his head above water.

A Daring Rescue

Officer Trostle and Gabe carefully walked onto the ice to rescue Porter. They held out a long tree branch for Porter to grab with his mouth. However, the ice broke before they could reach him. Both rescuers crashed into the water. After the pair climbed out, police at the scene tried to help Porter. They tossed a long cord around the dog's neck to pull him to shore—but their efforts also failed.

In one last attempt, Officer Trostle crawled back onto the ice and called to Porter. As she inched closer to him, the ice once again collapsed, and she fell back into the water. This time, however, the dog swam straight to her. "I think he knew I was there to help him," said Officer Trostle. The exhausted pair swam back to shore. Despite being cold and wet, Officer Trostle, Gabe, and Porter were all fine—and thankful to be alive.

Officer Trostle crawled onto the ice on her belly and fell into the water a second time.

Gabe's grandmother, Sue, dried off Porter after he was rescued.

 A newspaper reporter at the scene made a video of Officer Trostle's rescue of Porter. The story spread quickly and was aired on state and national news programs.

Different Duties

For Jane Trostle and other animal control officers, rescuing animals is a regular part of their job. However, they also have other duties. The officers help sick, injured, or **abused** animals. In addition, they **patrol** streets, parks, and other public areas for lost or **stray animals**. If officers find a stray, they bring it to an **animal shelter**, where it will be cared for.

Animal control officer Jennifer Trotter with a lost dog that she has caught

Animal control officers also look for animals that are dangerous to people. When wild or **domesticated animals** bite or try to attack people, officers race to the scene. It's their job to safely capture the creatures. They will also make sure the animals are checked for diseases, such as **rabies**, that could harm people or pets.

 It is **illegal** to keep a wild animal as a pet unless the owner has a special **permit**. Animal control officers are responsible for removing illegal pets from people's homes.

Officer Will Luna and a young deer that was kept as an illegal pet

Job Training

Since animal control officers perform many duties, their job requires special training. Many officers have taken college classes in **zoology**. Others have received a special **certification** or spent years working at animal shelters, **kennels**, or **veterinary clinics**.

Before becoming animal control officers, many job applicants spend time learning about and caring for animals.

When people first begin working as animal control officers, they usually go through an on-the-job training program. They watch experienced officers at work to learn how to handle all types of animals—from kittens to snakes. Officers are also trained to capture or rescue animals using special equipment, such as a **snare pole**. Most of all, they are taught to think on their feet. Why? "Officers never know what kind of situation may occur," said one longtime animal control officer.

Officer Roger Underwood holds a beaver that he caught in downtown Galesburg, Illinois. The beaver was later released into a nearby lake.

 Animal control officers usually work for a town, city, or county government. They are required to learn all local and state laws that relate to animals.

Down the Drain

Even with a lot of training, animal control officers still face surprises on the job. In June 2012, Officer Anthony Cills was called to the Fairfield Inn in Millville, New Jersey, after an inn guest heard chirps coming from a large **storm drain**. The officer soon discovered that six baby wild turkeys had tumbled through the **grate** and were stuck at the bottom of the drain.

Turkeys are often seen on the grounds of the Fairfield Inn in Millville, New Jersey.

With help from other rescuers, the heavy grate was removed, and Cills jumped into the drain. He immediately rescued four of the fluffy babies. However, the two remaining birds ran farther into the drainpipes. To **coax** the babies out, the rescuers tapped on the pipes and used turkey calls. The birds didn't budge. After working for two hours, Officer Cills safely captured the last two baby turkeys.

Officer Cills trying to get the last baby turkey out of the storm drain

After the rescue, Officer Cills hoped to return the six baby turkeys to their mother. However, she could not be found. Instead, the birds were taken to a special wildlife animal shelter.

A baby wild turkey

Night Crawler

Animal control officers may be called upon at any time, day or night. In 2008, Officer Bruce Dangerfield of Vero Beach, Florida, received an emergency call at 2:00 in the morning. The sheriff's office told him that a huge snake has been spotted slithering through a neighborhood—and Dangerfield needed to catch it!

Animal control officer
Bruce Dangerfield

Dangerfield jumped into his van and drove around, keeping an eye out for the stray snake. He soon located the 10-foot (3 m) long red-tailed **boa constrictor**. Using his bare hands, he carefully grabbed the back of the snake's head to prevent it from biting him. Then he placed the enormous animal in a large sack in his van. Officer Dangerfield took the snake to his house to care for it until he could find the hissing giant a home.

 Many people buy small baby boa constrictors as pets, not realizing how big and dangerous they can become. Adult boas can reach 13 feet (4 m) and can easily kill a cat or dog.

Officer Dangerfield with the boa constrictor he caught, which was likely an escaped pet

A Chimney Hideaway

Why do stray animals need to be caught? One fear is that they may carry deadly diseases that could spread to people or other animals. Officer Bill Lehman of Clifton Park, New York, once **tracked** a raccoon that had crawled down a homeowner's chimney. The officer worried that the animal might have rabies.

Raccoons, such as this one, often go into chimneys because a chimney, like a hollow tree, can be a safe, warm place to live and to raise young.

 Rabies is a deadly disease that is spread by **infected** animals. In the past, rabies was usually passed on though dog bites. In recent years, however, more rabies cases have come from the bites of infected raccoons, skunks, and bats.

To reach the raccoon, Officer Lehman scrambled up the roof and then stuck a snare pole down the chimney. For more than an hour, he tried to catch the frisky animal. Lehman began to suspect that the raccoon wasn't diseased, since sick animals are usually slow moving and easy to catch. He finally snared the raccoon—a large, healthy female. Afterwards, he set her free in an area far from people's homes.

An animal control officer releasing a raccoon

Caging a Coyote

A snare pole is one kind of tool that animal control officers use to capture stray creatures. Another helpful piece of equipment is a **live trap**. It came in handy in 2006, when residents of Oak Park, Illinois, spotted coyotes in their neighborhood. One of the animals was hiding under the **deck** of a house.

Coyotes are shy animals that hunt mostly mice and rabbits and rarely attack people.

In order to catch the coyote, animal control officer Jason Pounds placed a live trap under the deck. He put the wire cage in front of the coyote's only escape path. Then he gently poked the animal with a long pole. The coyote ran straight into the cage, which the officer quickly shut. Was the coyote a threat to residents of Oak Park? Officer Pounds didn't think so. The coyote was probably just looking for an easy meal in a nearby garbage can.

Officer Pounds and the caged coyote

The trapped coyote was released in a forest **preserve** far from Oak Park.

The Long Chase

Not all animals are caught as quickly and easily as the coyote in Oak Park. In February 2007, animal control officer Valerie Schomburg got a call to rescue a dog that had been **abandoned** by its owner outside a hotel in Santa Ana, California. The officer hoped to rescue the dog, named Cooper, before a car hit him.

Stray dogs near streets and highways are in danger of being hit by cars.

Officer Schomburg set out bits of meat to attract the **canine**. However, Cooper ran away whenever the officer approached him. For months, Schomburg tried to catch the dog, but he always fled. Finally, in May, a person who had heard about Cooper's story caught the dog and took him to a shelter. Amazingly, that same night, Cooper chewed his way through a metal fence and escaped from the shelter. Luckily, Cooper was caught by another animal control officer a week later.

Cooper with Officer Schomburg, who never gave up trying to catch and save the dog she calls Super Duper Cooper.

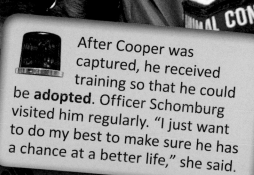

After Cooper was captured, he received training so that he could be **adopted**. Officer Schomburg visited him regularly. "I just want to do my best to make sure he has a chance at a better life," she said.

A Deadly Match

Cooper was rescued after his owner had abandoned him. Sometimes, however, officers rescue animals whose owners abuse them. David Grow is an animal control officer in Michigan who has rescued dogs that were used for dogfighting.

An injured pit bull that had been used by its owner for dogfighting

Dogfighting is an illegal sport in which owners force their dogs to fight. Dogfights are usually held in secret places such as back alleys or basements. People then bet on whichever dog they think will win. During the fight, the dogs often hurt one another. Sometimes, the injuries are deadly.

In 2011, Officer Grow was able to rescue seven dogs from a fight. Unfortunately, two still died from their injuries. Yet thanks to David Grow and other animal control officers like him, many fighting dogs are rescued and given a chance for a new life.

Officer Grow places a dog rescued from a dogfight into his truck.

 People who run dogfights train their dogs to be tough. Sometimes they even starve them to make them more **aggressive**.

Double Trouble

Every day, animal control officers may put themselves in danger. Just ask Officer Jacqueline Lynch of Longview, Texas. In 2012, she responded to a report about a loose pit bull behind a home. As she was trying to capture the pit bull, she heard the sounds of another pit bull approaching. Before she could escape, both dogs attacked her and bit her right hand.

One of the dogs jumped over a backyard fence in order to attack Officer Lynch.

Officer Jacqueline Lynch

Seeking safety, Officer Lynch ran to a house across the street. The snarling dogs bolted after her. The owner of the house said, "She came into my door, and I pushed her in." Luckily, the homeowner saved Lynch from being attacked again. The officer was then taken to a **clinic**, where she was treated for her bites. The pit bulls were eventually captured by other animal control officers.

One of the pit bulls after it was captured

After they were captured, the dogs that attacked animal control officer Lynch were put in a holding pen for ten days to make sure they weren't carrying rabies.

Why Be an Animal Control Officer?

An animal control officer has a dangerous job. So why would anyone want to do it? Growing up, Travis Trexler often watched television ads that spoke out against animal cruelty. The pictures of abused animals that he saw bothered him. As a result, Trexler became an officer in Fairbanks, Alaska. He wanted to do his part to help animals in need.

There are about 15,000 animal control officers in the United States.

An animal control officer with a rescued kitten

Melissa Douglas was a **vet technician** before becoming an animal control officer in Bowie, Maryland. She believes that animals know when people are trying to help them. "They understand more than we think," she said. "If they feel they can trust a human, their behavior changes." Thanks to the heroic acts and the dedication of these officers, many animals and people live better, safer lives.

Animal control officer Amaka Watson holds a baby rabbit.

Animal Control Officers' Equipment

Animal control officers use many different kinds of equipment when catching animals.

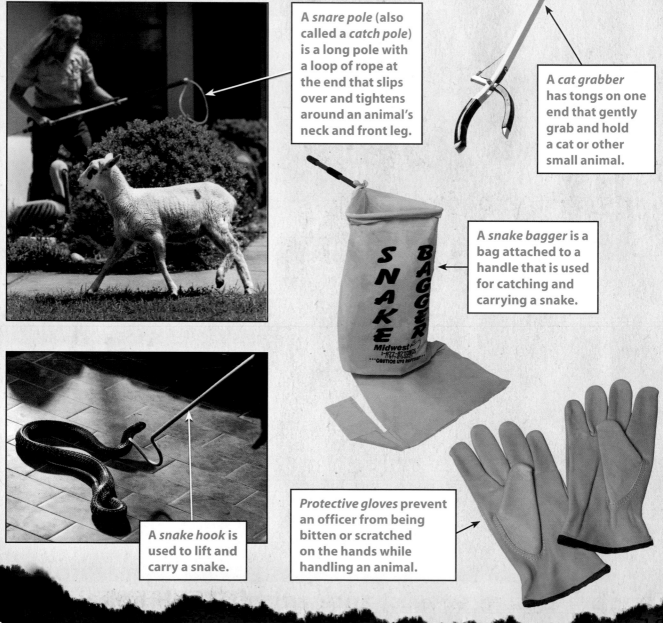

A *snare pole* (also called a *catch pole*) is a long pole with a loop of rope at the end that slips over and tightens around an animal's neck and front leg.

A *cat grabber* has tongs on one end that gently grab and hold a cat or other small animal.

A *snake bagger* is a bag attached to a handle that is used for catching and carrying a snake.

A *snake hook* is used to lift and carry a snake.

Protective gloves prevent an officer from being bitten or scratched on the hands while handling an animal.

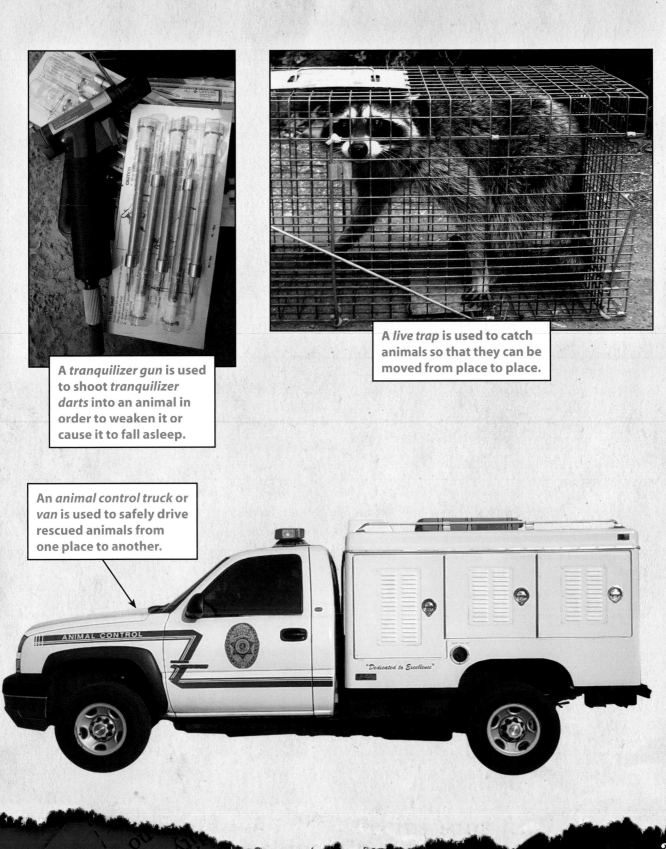

A *tranquilizer gun* is used to shoot *tranquilizer darts* into an animal in order to weaken it or cause it to fall asleep.

A *live trap* is used to catch animals so that they can be moved from place to place.

An *animal control truck* or *van* is used to safely drive rescued animals from one place to another.

ANIMAL CONTROL

"Dedicated to Excellence"

Glossary

abandoned (uh-BAN-duhnd) left alone and uncared for; deserted

abused (uh-BYOOZD) treated badly or cruelly

adopted (uh-DOPT-id) taken in as part of one's family

aggressive (uh-GRESS-iv) behaving in a fierce or threatening way

animal shelter (AN-uh-muhl SHEL-tur) a place where homeless or unwanted animals can stay

boa constrictor (BOH-uh kuhn-STRIK-tur) a kind of snake that kills its prey by coiling around it and squeezing tightly

canine (KAY-nine) a member of the dog family

certification (sur-tuh-fuh-KAY-shun) the condition of meeting special training requirements for a specific job

clinic (KLIN-ik) a place, usually smaller than a hospital, where people go for medical treatment

coax (KOHKS) to gently persuade someone to do something

deck (DEK) a raised platform on the outside of a house or building

domesticated animals (duh-MESS-tuh-*kayt*-id AN-uh-muhlz) animals that have been tamed so that they can live with people, such as dogs and cats

grate (GRAYT) a type of metal frame that covers an opening

illegal (i-LEE-guhl) against the law

infected (in-FEK-tid) having a disease caused by germs

kennels (KEN-uhlz) places where dogs or cats are raised, trained, and looked after

live trap (LIVE TRAP) a container made of metal bars that is used to trap animals and move them from place to place

patrol (puh-TROHL) to travel around an area to protect it

permit (PUR-mit) a document giving someone permission to do something

preserve (pri-ZURV) a place where animals are protected

rabies (RAY-beez) an often deadly disease, spread by the bite of an animal, that can affect humans, dogs, bats, and other warm-blooded animals

shore (SHOR) the land along the edge of an ocean, river, or lake

snare pole (SNAIR POHL) a long tool with a looped rope on one end that is used to catch animals

storm drain (STORM DRAYN) a pipe or pipes that take away excess water after heavy rain

stray animals (STRAY AN-uh-muhlz) animals without owners

tracked (TRAKT) followed someone or something

vet technician (VET tek-NISH-uhn) someone who works with special equipment, often in a laboratory, to study or help animals

veterinary clinics (VET-ur-uhn-*er*-ee KLIN-iks) places where sick or injured animals are treated and cared for

zoology (zoh-OL-uh-jee) the scientific study of animals

Bibliography

Aronson, Stephen. *Animal Control Management: A New Look at a Public Responsibility.* West Lafayette, IN: Purdue University Press (2010).

Duffy-Korpics, Lisa. *Tales from a Dog Catcher.* Guilford, CT: Lyons Press (2009).

Rogers, Tom. *A Working Guide to Animal Control and Enforcement.* Frederick, MD: PublishAmerica (2009).

Read More

Best Friends Animal Society. *Not Left Behind: Rescuing the Pets of New Orleans.* New York: Yorkville Press (2006).

Goldish, Meish. *Wildlife Rehabilitators to the Rescue (The Work of Heroes: First Responders in Action).* New York: Bearport (2013).

Somerville, Bob. *The Cats of Kittyville: New Lives for Rescued Felines.* South Portland, ME: Sellers Publishing (2008).

Somerville, Bob. *Dogtown: A Sanctuary for Rescued Dogs.* South Portland, ME: Sellers Publishing (2008).

Learn More Online

To learn more about animal control officers, visit
www.bearportpublishing.com/TheWorkofHeroes

Index

About the Author

Meish Goldish has written more than 200 books for children.
His book *Army: Civilian to Soldier* was a Children's Choices Selection in 2012.
He lives in Brooklyn, New York.

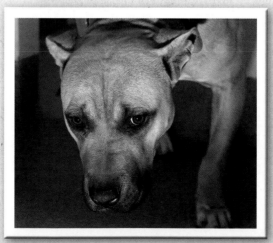